WINNIPEG JETS

BY ETHAN OLSON

Book design by Maggie Villaume
Cover design by Maggie Villaume

Photographs ©: Matt Patterson/AP Images, cover; Steve Roberts/Cal Sport Media/ZUMA Press/AP Images, 4–5, 7; Mark Humphrey/AP Images, 8; Erik S. Lesser/AP Images, 10–11; Gregory Smith/AP Images, 12; Keith Srakocic/AP Images, 15; Andy Blenkush/Cal Sport Media/AP Images, 16–17; Trevor Hagan/The Canadian Press/AP Images, 19, 21, 24–25; Tony Gutierrez/AP Images, 22–23; John Woods/The Canadian Press/AP Images, 27; Jack Dempsey/AP Images, 28

Press Box Books, an imprint of Press Room Editions.

ISBN
978-1-63494-682-7 (library bound)
978-1-63494-706-0 (paperback)
978-1-63494-752-7 (epub)
978-1-63494-730-5 (hosted ebook)

Library of Congress Control Number: 2022919589

Distributed by North Star Editions, Inc.
2297 Waters Drive
Mendota Heights, MN 55120
www.northstareditions.com

Printed in the United States of America
Mankato, MN
082023

ABOUT THE AUTHOR
Ethan Olson is a sportswriter and editor based in Minneapolis.

TABLE OF CONTENTS

1

Mark Scheifele tallied 11 points in the seven-game playoff series against the Nashville Predators in 2018.

THE SOARING JETS

By the 2017–18 season, the Jets had been in Winnipeg, Manitoba, for seven years. Their first six hadn't seen much success. But Winnipeg was a force in 2017–18. The Jets finished with the second most points in the National Hockey League (NHL). Then they beat the Minnesota Wild in the first round of the playoffs. That set up a series with the Nashville Predators. They were the only team with more points than Winnipeg that season. A tight series was expected. The teams traded wins through six games. That set up a winner-take-all seventh game.

Game 7 was in Nashville's Bridgestone Arena. Loud fans packed the stands. But the Jets calmed the crowd down early. They scored two goals in the opening 11 minutes. Winnipeg went into the first intermission leading 2–1.

The Jets held on to that lead for most of the second period. With three minutes left in the period, the Predators sprung an attack. Nashville winger Kevin Fiala got the puck in a dangerous position. He deked by a defender and got in front of the net. However, Winnipeg goalie

Connor Hellebuyck makes one of his 36 saves in Game 7 against the Predators.

Connor Hellebuyck blocked Fiala's shot with his chest.

Less than a minute later, Winnipeg left winger Kyle Connor carried the puck

The Jets spill over the bench after defeating the Predators in Game 7.

into Nashville's zone. The puck was
poked off his stick. But teammate Blake
Wheeler got to it first. Wheeler found an
open Mark Scheifele with a perfect pass.

Then Scheifele slapped a one-timer into the back of the net.

The Predators couldn't come back from that. They fought to get back in the game. But Hellebuyck stopped 36 of the 37 shots he faced. The Jets went on to win 5–1. Winnipeg fans had endured a lot over the years, including the original Jets team moving away in 1996. Those difficult days were over. The new Jets were headed to the conference finals.

WINNIPEG WHITE OUT

The "Winnipeg White Out" became a playoff tradition for the original Winnipeg Jets. Their fans wore all white for each home game in the first round of the 1987 playoffs. The Jets beat the Calgary Flames that year. The new Winnipeg Jets brought the tradition back for the 2018 playoffs. And it boosted the team once again.

2

Ray Ferraro was Atlanta's captain in the 2001–02 season.

ATLANTA
ORIGINS

The NHL was growing in the late 1990s. Four new teams entered the league in a span of three seasons. The city of Atlanta, Georgia, became home to one of those teams. The Atlanta Thrashers played their first season in 1999–2000. But the team struggled early on.

The Thrashers won 56 games in their first three seasons. All the losing earned them multiple high

Dany Heatley tallied 181 points in 190 games with Atlanta.

draft picks. The Thrashers took winger

Dany Heatley second overall in the 2000

draft. A year later, they drafted winger

Ilya Kovalchuk first overall. Both players debuted in the 2001–02 season. Heatley won the Calder Memorial Trophy after recording 67 points. The Calder is given to the league's best rookie. Kovalchuk finished second in voting behind his teammate.

The added talent led to more wins. But the Thrashers continued to miss the playoffs. That changed in 2006–07. Right winger Marián Hossa formed a dangerous duo with Kovalchuk. They combined to

NASTY NEST

Atlanta's fans were known to shout and distract other teams' players. Eventually, a section of season ticket holders took on the name the "Nasty Nest." The name stuck. And the fans made Atlanta's Philips Arena a tough place for opposing teams to visit.

score 85 goals that season. And they led Atlanta to its first playoff appearance. But the success didn't last long. The Thrashers lost in a sweep in the first round. They never made it back to the playoffs in Atlanta. By 2010–11, many fans had lost interest. As a result, the team was losing money. The Thrashers had to find a new home.

Winnipeg had been home to an NHL team before. The original Jets played there from 1979 to 1996. But that team moved to Arizona and changed its name to the Coyotes. Now Winnipeg had a chance to bring the Thrashers north. A group called True North Sports and Entertainment put together a deal to buy

Ilya Kovalchuk (17) skates around Mario Lemieux of the Pittsburgh Penguins during an October 2005 game.

the team in 2011. The league approved the move later that year. Finally, the NHL was back in Winnipeg.

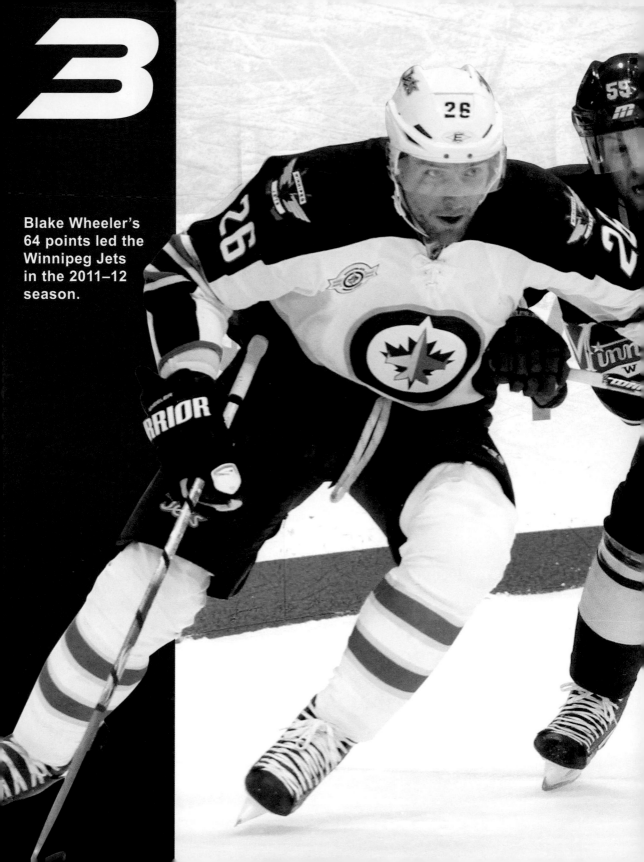

3

Blake Wheeler's 64 points led the Winnipeg Jets in the 2011–12 season.

BACK IN
WINNIPEG

When the team arrived in Winnipeg in 2011, it took on the old Jets nickname. Fans were ready. Season tickets for the 2011–12 season sold out in 17 minutes. Now the Jets could focus on piling up talent.

The Jets had traded for winger Blake Wheeler in 2011 while still in Atlanta. The rising star was someone to build around. Captain Andrew Ladd and defenseman

Dustin Byfuglien also joined the team that year. That duo had just won the Stanley Cup with the Chicago Blackhawks.

The Jets improved in their new home. But they missed the playoffs in each of their first three seasons. Wheeler continued to improve quickly. He led the team in points for two of the first three years in Winnipeg.

The NHL changed its divisions to help with travel before the 2013–14 season. The Jets moved to the

AN EXPENSIVE DEBUT

The return to Winnipeg came with a price. The fans were excited for their home opener against the Montreal Canadiens in 2011. That made ticket prices skyrocket. Secondhand tickets sold for an average of $713. The remaining Jets games that month sold for an average of $173.

Dustin Byfuglien (33) was known for his physical play.

Western Conference. And they joined the Central Division. But they still fell short of the playoffs. The Jets finished last in their division in 2013–14 despite winning 37 games.

During the season, the team fired head coach Claude Noel. His replacement was the experienced Paul Maurice. He had been coaching in the league for 15 years. The Jets improved in the final 35 games under Maurice. That gave fans hope for the future.

Maurice's first full season in Winnipeg was even better. The Jets made the playoffs for the first time since their move from Atlanta. They finished the regular season with 99 points. That was the most in team history at the time. However, the playoffs proved to be a problem. The Jets were swept in the first round by the Anaheim Ducks. But Maurice had the team headed in the right direction.

Andrew Ladd (16) celebrates after Tyler Myers (57) scored in the 2015 playoffs against the Anaheim Ducks.

BLAKE WHEELER

Blake Wheeler started his career with the Boston Bruins. The right winger only got better when he was traded to the Atlanta Thrashers in 2011. Following the team's move to Winnipeg that summer, no player became more attached to the Jets than Wheeler.

Wheeler was a model of consistency for Winnipeg. His leadership earned him the role of captain in 2016. He became known for his vision on the ice. Wheeler was a master at setting up his teammates. He led the NHL with 68 assists in the 2017–18 season. That helped him become the Jets' all-time points leader in 2019.

Wheeler was at his best when it mattered most. He had 18 assists in 17 playoff games in 2018. That helped the Jets make their deep run

Blake Wheeler has led the Jets in assists in five separate seasons.

4

Right wing Patrik Laine finished second in Calder Memorial Trophy voting in the 2016–17 season.

MAURICE'S MAGIC

The Jets fell back into a slump after the 2015 playoffs. They finished last in their division the next season. The team began making moves to try to improve.

Captain Andrew Ladd was traded to the Chicago Blackhawks just days before the 2016 trade deadline. Blake Wheeler took over as captain. The Jets also drafted winger Patrik Laine second overall in the 2016 draft. The Finnish teenager was an instant success. Laine was only 18 years old. But he finished third on the team with 64 points in the 2016–17 season.

By 2017–18, the Jets were back in the playoffs. Their 114 points that season were the most in team history. They also finished second in the NHL in goals with 277. After winning two playoff series, the Jets made their first appearance in the conference finals. The Vegas Golden Knights were waiting for them. Dustin Byfuglien got things going early for Winnipeg. The defenseman ripped a slap shot into the net 65 seconds into Game 1.

The Jets gather around Dustin Byfuglien to celebrate his goal in Game 1 of the 2018 Western Conference finals.

Laine tucked away a power play goal less than six minutes later.

The Jets ended Game 1 with a 4–2 win. But the Golden Knights picked

Kyle Connor led the Jets in points during the 2021–22 season, finishing with 93.

themselves up. They rallied to win the series in five games. The most successful season in team history was over.

The Jets made the playoffs in the following three years. But they could never repeat 2018. Paul Maurice stepped down during the 2021–22 season. He believed that the Jets would be better with a new coach. But they ended up missing the playoffs that year. The team still had players like Wheeler and talented winger Kyle Connor. Winnipeg fans remained hopeful their team could go on another playoff run.

NEW LEADERSHIP

Rick Bowness became the Winnipeg coach in 2022. He quickly shook things up. Bowness decided that the Jets would play without a captain. He wanted to focus on building more team-based leadership. That meant, for the first time since 2016, Blake Wheeler no longer wore the "C" on his jersey.

● WINNIPEG JETS
QUICK STATS

TEAM HISTORY: Atlanta Thrashers (1999–2011), Winnipeg Jets (2011–)

STANLEY CUP CHAMPIONSHIPS: 0*

KEY COACHES:

- Bob Hartley (2003–07): 136 wins, 118 losses, 13 ties, 24 overtime losses

- Claude Noel (2011–14): 80 wins, 79 losses, 18 overtime losses

- Paul Maurice (2014–21): 315 wins, 224 losses, 62 overtime losses

HOME ARENA: Canada Life Centre (Winnipeg, MB)

MOST CAREER POINTS: Blake Wheeler (757)

MOST CAREER GOALS: Ilya Kovalchuk (328)

MOST CAREER ASSISTS: Blake Wheeler (511)

MOST CAREER SHUTOUTS: Connor Hellebuyck (28)

Stats are accurate through the 2021–22 season.

GLOSSARY

ASSIST
A pass, rebound, or deflection that results in a goal.

CAPTAIN
A team's leader.

DEBUT
First appearance.

DEKE
To fake a movement in a certain direction to confuse an opponent.

DRAFT
An event that allows teams to choose new players coming into the league.

ONE-TIMER
A shot that a player takes immediately after receiving a pass, without controlling the puck first.

ROOKIE
A first-year player.

SWEEP
When a team wins all the games in a series.

TO LEARN MORE

BOOKS

Davidson, B. Keith. *NHL*. New York: Crabtree Publishing, 2022.

Doeden, Matt. *G.O.A.T. Hockey Teams*. Minneapolis: Lerner Publications, 2021.

Duling, Kaitlyn. *Women in Hockey*. Lake Elmo, MN: Focus Readers, 2020.

MORE INFORMATION

To learn more about the Winnipeg Jets, go to **pressboxbooks.com/AllAccess**.

These links are routinely monitored and updated to provide the most current information available.

INDEX